27 IRISH EMPLO... CASE...

PRICELESS LESSONS FOR EMPLOYERS AND EMPLOYEES FROM DECIDED CASES OF THE EAT, EQUALITY TRIBUNAL, AND HIGH COURT

By Terry Gorry B.Comm, Solicitor

Free Gift

As a way of saying thanks to my readers, I offer a free gift.

Get my free report, "**The 16 Common Employment Law Mistakes that Most Irish Employers Make**", and my regular money saving employment law tips via email.

At http://EmploymentRightsIreland.com

COPYRIGHT

All rights reserved. No part of this publication may be reproduced, distributed, or transmitted in any form or by any means, including photocopying, recording, or other electronic or mechanical methods , without the prior written permission of the publisher, except in the case of brief quotations embodied in critical reviews and certain other non-commercial uses permitted by copyright law.

For permission requests, contact the publisher at: Terry Gorry, Terry Gorry & Co. Solicitors, Enfield, Co. Meath, Ireland.

Text copyright © 2015 Terry Gorry

All Rights Reserved

DISCLAIMER

Although the author and publisher have made every effort to ensure that the information in this book was correct at press time, the author and publisher do not assume and hereby disclaim any liability to any party for any loss, damage, or disruption caused by errors or omissions, whether such errors or omissions result from negligence, accident, or any other cause.

The material contained in this book is provided for general information purposes only and does not constitute legal or other professional advice. Whilst every care has been taken in the preparation of the content of all pages in this book, specific legal advice should always be sought on the application of the law in any particular situation.

We strongly recommend employing a legal professional to interpret and advice on ANY aspect of the law.

INTRODUCTION

Are you an employer who's worried about employment related claims from employees?

Or an employee who's not sure whether you have a reasonable chance of succeeding with a claim?

Employment law in Ireland is a huge, complex subject. It's made up of common law, statute, regulations, EU directives, custom and practice, etc.

It's perfectly understandable why you could not keep on top of it all. Especially if you are running a business, or working in a busy job.

That's why this book should help.

Because it looks at actual decided cases, from 2010 to 2014, from the bodies who decide the winners and losers of employment cases: the Employment Appeals Tribunal (EAT), the Equality Authority, and the Courts (the High Court).

I take a look at 27 actual cases-22 from the EAT, 2 from the Equality Tribunal, and 3 from the High Court-and look at the lessons to be learned from them. I also provide a link to the original full decision of 24 of them.

The cases cover a wide range of topics, and involve real people in real workplace situations. Cases like the 'Stale Chicken Wrap' case, the 'Missing Jam Tarts' case, the case of the public transport employee who spat at a customer who was abusing her, the Special Needs Assistant in a Kildare primary school awarded over €250,000 in the High Court for bullying/personal injuries, the fast food restaurant manager who 'forgot to pay for his food', the security guard at a shopping centre fired for taking money from shopping centre parking pay stations, and more.

So, this book is not a dry statement of what the law states.

No, it takes the decisions from the actual decision makers and sees what they have to say about their decisions, how they arrived at those decisions, and the lessons you can learn from them.

The cases I look at are concerned with a wide range of issues, such as:

1. Gross misconduct

2. Discrimination

3. Temporary agency work

4. Tupe

5. Unfair dismissal

6. Constructive dismissal

7. Redundancy

8. Appeals and time limits

9. Bullying and personal injury

10. Independent contractor/employee

11. Settlement agreements

12. Long term sick/incapacity terminations

By the end of this book, you will have a very clear insight into how these types of cases are decided.

And, more importantly, the chances of your particular case being won or lost, or whether you should bring or defend an employment related claim.

How the cases are categorised in this book

There is a certain amount of crossover in many of the cases I look at. By this I mean that a case could easily be categorised under more than one category eg redundancy and unfair dismissal or discrimination and unfair dismissal.

I have tried to include the case under its predominant or most obvious category.

Table of Contents

Introduction

Table of Contents

1. The Problem with "Gross Misconduct" Dismissals

    The Stale Chicken Wrap Case

    Missing Jam Tarts Leads to "Fair and Proportionate" Dismissals Because of "Reasonable" Zero Tolerance Policy

    Dunnes Stores Manager Sacked for Gross Misconduct Wins €16,630 for Unfair Dismissal

    Public Transport Employee Dismissed for "Gross Misconduct" Wins Reinstatement

    Child Care Worker Dismissed for "Gross Misconduct" Awarded €19,000 for Unfair Dismissal

2. Discrimination

    Failure to Accommodate Employee's Return to Work on Part Time Basis Costs Employer €40,000

    Termination of Employment on Grounds of Incapacity-2 Vitally Important Long Term Sick Leave Cases

    De Sousa V Kepak Group

    Eugena Carroll and H.J. Heinz Frozen & Chilled Foods Limited

3. Temporary Agency Workers

    Forklift Driver Wins Over €20,000 Under New Temporary Agency Work Legislation

4. Transfer of Undertakings (TUPE)

    Static Guard Awarded €11,500 under TUPE (Protection of Employees on Transfer of Undertakings) Regulations

5. Unfair Dismissals

    Montessori Teacher Awarded €32,500 for Unfair Dismissal in Kildare

Unfair Selection for Redundancy-Awarded €50,000 for Unfair Dismissal

Creche Worker's Week Cut from 5 Days to 3-Wins €10,000 for Constructive Dismissal

Unfair Selection of Warehouse Operative for Redundancy-Awarded Compensation of €8,000

Abrekbabra Supervisor Awarded €9,500 For Unfair Dismissal-'Forgot to Pay' for Food

Mechanic Fails in Constructive Dismissal Claim-Burden of Proof 'Very High'

Security Officer Denied Taking Money from Shopping Centre Pay Stations-Wins €46,800 for Unfair Dismissal

Unfair Selection for Redundancy Claim Fails-€10,000 Ex Gratia Payment Offer Rejected

FAS Community Employment Employee Wins Unfair Dismissal Case and is Reinstated

Secondary School Secretary Awarded €9,850 for Unfair Dismissal

Pregnant Woman who Suffered Still Birth Awarded €72,000 for Unfair Dismissal

6. Time Limits

Employer Loses Appeal against Rights Commissioner Award of €8,000 Wages Due to Employee

7. Redundancy

Construction Worker's Claim of Unfair Selection for Redundancy Fails

8. Bullying and Workplace/Occupational Stress

Bullied in Primary School-Special Needs Assistant Awarded €255,000

Bullying and Workplace Stress as a Personal Injury-a Notable High Court Decision in 2014

9. Independent Contractor or Employee?

   The Crucial Significance in an Unfair Dismissal Case

10. Settlement Agreements

    Avoid This Costly Mistake in Your Employment Settlement Agreement

About the author

1. The Problem with "Gross Misconduct" Dismissals

Tribunals and Courts have often struggled to deliver consistent decisions around dismissal cases involving gross misconduct, and misconduct generally. The frustration for employers is that there is no clear cut definition or recognition of what will justify dismissal on this ground of "gross misconduct".

Let's take a look at 4 misconduct cases and the apparent difference in the decisions.

The Stale Chicken Wrap Case

Gate Gourmet had a contract supplying airline food to various airlines. In 2012 they received a complaint that one of their customers had been supplied with an out of date and stale chicken wrap; in fact, the wrap was out of date in February, 2012 and the complaint received in April, 2012.

Gate Gourmet's contract with this customer was to expire in July 2012 and this incident made it very difficult to ensure the contract was renewed. So, they took it very seriously and launched an investigation.

A preliminary investigation was undertaken by the branch manager at the date of the incident which led to the claimant's dismissal. The investigation was confined to how the out of date product had been supplied to the customer and the investigator had no role in making a recommendation in relation to the disciplinary process. However, the investigation concluded that the disciplinary procedure should be invoked on the grounds that the claimant had failed to comply with "in house" policies in relation to monitoring out of date stock.

On the 8 May 2012, the claimant attended a disciplinary hearing conducted by the production and purchasing manager. Prior to the hearing date, the claimant was notified by letter dated the 2 May 2012, that following a full investigation, four allegations against him would be included on the agenda as follows:

1. Failure to comply with standard operating procedures in the store area

2. Failure to implement appropriate processes to monitor stock rotation

3. Very serious breach of food safety standards

4. Failure to effectively supervise the stores with significant potential risk to public safety as well as to create serious damage to customer relations with the airline affected.

This worker was found to have failed to follow standard operating procedure, and was dismissed for gross misconduct on the grounds that the company took incidences such as this very seriously.

Two other employees also failed to notice the out of date wrap and received final written warnings. This different treatment from the treatment experienced by the sacked worker was something that was noted by the EAT.

The dismissed employee told the EAT that another worker actually took responsibility for not checking and recording the product, in accordance with procedures.

Decision of Tribunal
"The Tribunal is of the view that the appointment of the purchasing and production manager to conduct the disciplinary hearing in relation to the four allegations against the claimant was unfair and contrary to the principles of natural justice given that EK had a day to day operational function within the respondent company and ultimate responsibility for the stock and stores department. Furthermore, EK headed an investigation into the current stock control procedures, the results of

which formed the basis of the allegations against the claimant and in the absence of any evidence to the contrary, it appears that EK made the decision to dismiss.

The Tribunal finds that it was unfair and unreasonable to conclude that the claimant was solely and exclusively responsible for such failure. Termination of employment on the grounds of gross misconduct was a disproportionate sanction in all the circumstances, particularly but not exclusively taking into account that the claimant was employed by the company for a period of nineteen years with an unblemished record and the claimant received no formal verbal or written warning in the time preceding the incident and other personnel investigated received only final written warnings following the conclusion of the investigative process."

The EAT awarded him €45,000 for unfair dismissal and €5,889 in lieu of 8 weeks' notice to which he would have been entitled.

The worker had a blemish free record for 19 years and the Employment Appeals Tribunal decided that the sanction of dismissal was 'a disproportionate sanction in all the circumstances'.

Lesson

This case demonstrates once again that what is considered to be "gross misconduct" can vary from situation to situation and will be largely determined by the circumstances of each case.

Further lessons to be learned include the need to afford fair procedures and natural justice to the employee, regardless of the apparent seriousness of the conduct, and the need to consider alternatives to dismissal because the EAT looks very closely at the proportionality of the sanction imposed. In this case the sanction was described as "disproportionate".

This case can be contrasted with the "Missing Jam Tarts" case below.

Read the full decision:
http://www.workplacerelations.ie/en/Cases/2014/November/UD1195_2012_MN737_2012.html

Missing Jam Tarts Leads to "Fair and Proportionate" Dismissals Because of "Reasonable" Zero Tolerance Policy

This case was an appeal to the Employment Appeals Tribunal of a Rights Commissioner decision which had decided the two men involved were fairly dismissed.

The background to the case is the 2 employees worked for Keelings' Logistics Solutions who operated as a distribution company for the supply of goods to one customer. The 2 employees worked in Keelings' warehouse.

The security manager saw the 2 men "acting suspiciously" beside an open cage, and saw the cage being moved. He also said he saw the men eating something and putting their hands inside the cage, and stated the men had no business standing together in front of a cage.

The employer had a policy that no food would be consumed on the warehouse floor, and had installed vending machines on the shop floor to prevent staff tampering and/or eating stock.

The Warehouse Manager was alerted, and it became clear that a box containing jam tarts had been tampered with, and two individual tarts were missing from a packet.

An investigation was carried out which included CCTV footage, which was reviewed many times. The men, in their defence, said they were sharing a Mars bar and denied eating the jam tarts.

The employer carried out a disciplinary procedure and dismissed the men who appealed the decision but were unsuccessful.

The EAT found that the mens' evidence was not credible, and, on the balance of probability, that they did tamper with the stock.

The Tribunal also found that there were no procedural defects which would render the dismissal unfair. The investigation, disciplinary meetings, and appeal were thorough, fair and objective.

The Tribunal decision also stated:

"The Tribunal must assess where or not the sanction imposed was proportionate. The respondent stated that its function is to accept deliveries, process them and dispatch it to a third party stores. The third party is their only client and they are totally reliant on them for their business. There is a high level of trust between the respondent and the third party and that must be maintained at all times. If they tolerated staff tampering with stock the working relationship between them and the third party could be irretrievably damaged. That is why there is a zero tolerance policy. The respondent has placed vending machines on the shop floor to prevent staff tampering and/or eating stock. The Tribunal accepts that the respondent's zero tolerance policy is reasonable in the circumstances. Any dismissal arising out of a breach of the policy is fair and proportionate."

Lesson

What's interesting about this case is that the EAT found that the employer's zero tolerance policy in relation to staff tampering with stock was *"reasonable in the circumstances"*. Generally, it can be difficult to justify a zero tolerance policy.

Many cases similar to this one has seen the EAT finding that the response of the employer was excessive and disproportionate. For example, the "Stale Chicken Wrap" case above, or the case involving the rail transport worker who spat in the face of a member of the public, which I look at later in this chapter.

But, the fact that Keelings Logistics Solutions had only one customer and there was naturally a very high degree of trust required between them and their customer seems to have been critical in the EAT finding that the zero tolerance policy was reasonable in this case.

Read full decision here:
http://www.workplacerelations.ie/en/Cases/2014/November/UD828_2013.html

DUNNES STORES MANAGER SACKED FOR GROSS MISCONDUCT WINS €16,630 FOR UNFAIR DISMISSAL

This case involved a department manager with Dunnes Stores, who set up a side business selling goods from a cash and carry to colleagues.

The store manager had received a letter of complaint from a local community group. The complaint was that the department manager had opened an account in their name at a cash and carry. The community group's letterhead was used to validate the association with the group to open the account. The wife of one of the community group leaders worked for the respondent, and the wife of another community group leader worked for the cash and carry; hence the discovery and subsequent complaint.

As a result of this complaint, the store manager held a meeting with the claimant on the 11th of February 2012. The claimant admitted taking the community group's letter requesting a bag pack and doctoring it for the purposes of opening an account with the cash and carry. By way of explanation, the claimant said she was in financial difficulty and was earning extra money from selling the cash and carry goods. The meeting was adjourned.

Later that day, the meeting reconvened as a disciplinary meeting. The claimant was offered, and declined, representation. The claimant again admitted using the letter to open an account, but denied selling the goods to Dunnes Stores' staff. The claimant then admitted to selling the goods purchased on a different cash and carry account to staff in Dunnes Stores. The claimant was suspended until the 13th of February, 2012, and warned that the outcome of the disciplinary process could be dismissal.

At the disciplinary meeting on the 13th of February the store manager outlined the allegations as follows:

'1. Misrepresentation of the company

2. Forgery

3. Fraud'

The claimant again explained her very difficult personal circumstances that led to her actions. The store manager had been aware of her difficult circumstances prior to this incident. The meeting was adjourned for the store manager to consider the situation. The store manager then sought advice from the HR department during the disciplinary process. As per the respondent's disciplinary procedures, the claimant was dismissed for 'conduct, including social conduct unbecoming of an employee of the company or contrary to its best interest or which could bring the company reputation into disrepute.'

The store manager had *"thought long and hard about it over the weekend"*, so delivered his decision to dismiss the claimant when the meeting reconvened after a 15 minute break. The claimant was dismissed for gross misconduct, stating that, 'as far as I & the company are concerned the bond of trust has been irrevocably broken'.

He outlined the appeal process to the claimant. The letter of dismissal was issued to the claimant on the same day.

Dunnes position was that the claimant was a department manager and in a position of trust, and no other sanction would have been appropriate given the serious nature of the offence. The store manager did take the claimant's long service, clean disciplinary record, and family problems into consideration before making his decision.

Dunnes argued at the Employment Appeals Tribunal hearing that they had lost the fundamental trust required in the employer/employee relationship. The employee explained that she was in serious financial difficulty when she ran her "enterprise".

She had good service record of 10 years with Dunnes, and a clean disciplinary record. Dunnes claimed that they took both of these factors into account in their decision to dismiss.

The employee appealed the decision to dismiss, but it was upheld by a regional manager who said the essential element of trust was no longer possible in the employer/employee relationship. The regional manager told the hearing that the employee was an excellent employee, but the bond of trust was broken, so no lesser sanction would be appropriate for gross misconduct.

No appeal meeting was held as it was not the employer's policy; the appeal that was allowed involved a review of the documentation and disciplinary meeting notes.

Decision of the EAT

The Employment Appeals Tribunal took a different view:

"As this was the claimant's first offence, committed in a time of great personal difficulty which the respondent was aware of, the sanction of dismissal was disproportionate."

The employee was awarded €14,000 in compensation for unfair dismissal and an additional €2,630 under the Minimum Notice and Terms of Employment Acts 1973 to 2005.

Lesson

The question of proportionality was again considered by the EAT in this case, that is to say, was the sanction disproportionate?

This is a common question posed by the EAT in unfair dismissal cases: were other lesser sanctions more appropriate in the circumstances?

Clearly, it can be very difficult for employers to be sure whether a decision to terminate will subsequently be held to be fair or unfair.

Read the full decision here:
http://www.workplacerelations.ie/en/Cases/2014/May/UD517_2012_RP385_2012_MN396_2012.html

PUBLIC TRANSPORT EMPLOYEE DISMISSED FOR "GROSS MISCONDUCT" WINS REINSTATEMENT

This case involved a public transport service employee who spat at a member of the public, and was dismissed for "gross misconduct". The decision to dismiss her was upheld at a Rights Commissioner hearing in the 1st instance, and the employee then appealed her case to the Employment Appeals Tribunal.

Background
A member of the public was annoying other passengers on the public transport service, and the employee intervened. However, she was racially abused and spat at. The employee spat back at the passenger, and the entire exchange was recorded on CCTV.

The employee admitted she was at fault in the subsequent disciplinary process. The employer dismissed her for "gross misconduct", and the employee brought case to Rights Commissioner who found against her and felt the employer was justified in dismissing her.

In the appeal to Employment Appeals Tribunal, counsel for the employee appealed the "too severe" penalty, and pointed to her excellent prior record.

The EAT found that the dismissal was disproportionate and referred to section *6(1) of Unfair Dismissals act, 1977* which states:

"the dismissal of an employee shall be deemed, for the purposes of this Act, to be an unfair dismissal unless, having regard to all the circumstances, there were substantial grounds justifying the dismissal."

The EAT noted that "substantial grounds" are required to justify a dismissal. The EAT explained this as follows:

"The adjective "substantial" means that the ground relied upon should be a matter of substance rather than form, and should be a matter of gravity. In weighing the gravity of the matter against the penalty of dismissal the Tribunal must have "regard to all the circumstances" as the subsection requires. In other words the Tribunal should decide whether the penalty of dismissal is proportionate to the offence. The doctrine of proportionality is now well established in Irish law since Cox v Ireland (1992 2 I.R. 503) and Heaney v Ireland (1994 3 I.R. 593) and elaborated in other cases since then.

Having viewed the video of the event, the Tribunal is of the view that the conduct of the appellant was such as to bring the company into disrepute and would justify a penalty of some sort, but "having regard to all the circumstances" especially the severe provocation would not amount to "gross" misconduct as the respondent argued."

Interestingly the EAT noted:

"Subsection 6 (1) does not use the adjective "gross" or even the word "misconduct" but only the more neutral word "conduct." As already stated her conduct did merit some penalty, but the penalty should be proportionate. When we add in the element of provocation, and also have regard to her previous excellent record, we are of the view that dismissal was disproportionate."

The EAT found that appellant's conduct contributed to her dismissal, but decided nevertheless that she was to be re-engaged back into the position she previously held, and this was to take effect from 1st Jan. 2012. The period of absence from December 2010 to January 2012 was to be counted for continuous service, but not remuneration or leave entitlements.

Lesson

This case shows once again the difficulty for an employer in assessing "misconduct" or "conduct", as the EAT pointed out in its decision, in deciding appropriate and proportionate sanctions for unacceptable behaviour or conduct.

Read the full decision here: http://employmentlawireland.ie/wp-content/uploads/2013/08/public-transport-reinstatement.pdf

Child Care Worker Dismissed for "Gross Misconduct" Awarded €19,000 for Unfair Dismissal

This case is yet another case of dismissal by the employer on the grounds of the employee's alleged "gross misconduct". The worker was a child care worker in a creche.

She had failed to observe an incident involving bullying where 2 older boys put a sock in the mouth of another child. The child's father wanted an investigation. The claimant's position was that she might have been on a break and did not see the incident.

She was dismissed with immediate effect after the boy's father had put pressure on the manager of the creche.

It transpired that the claimant was on a break for 15 minutes, and that creche procedures were not followed resulting in a child being put at risk unnecessarily.

However, the manager did not inform the claimant that the meeting to which she was called was disciplinary. She was dismissed for bringing the crèche into disrepute.

The claimant was not advised of her right to appeal the decision, and the manager over-ruled the company disciplinary policy because, in the manager's view, the child's life had been in danger. The claimant was shocked to hear what had happened, but did not realize her job was in jeopardy prior to her dismissal.

She had not worked since her dismissal.

The EAT determined that the dismissal had been *"procedurally unfair, and the decision to dismiss lacked proportionality"*. The creche worker was awarded €19,000 for unfair dismissal.

Lesson

This case is yet another example of an employer losing an unfair dismissal case because the procedure followed in carrying out the dismissal was unfair, and lacked natural justice and fair procedures.

In addition, the decision lacked "proportionality", and this too is a common finding when an employee is dismissed for gross misconduct.

2. Discrimination

Failure to Accommodate Employee's Return to Work on Part Time Basis Costs Employer €40,000

This case concerned a man who worked in a quarry and who had suffered a brain tumour.

He brought a claim against his employer to the Equality Tribunal, on the grounds that he was discriminatorily dismissed from his job, and claimed that the employer failed to provide "reasonable accommodation" for his return to work.

Background

The man started working in the quarry in 2004. In 2009 he underwent surgery for a brain tumour and he made a full recovery. He was advised by his doctor that he would be fit to work for 20 hours per week.

The employer initially accepted this and accommodated him, and gave him 5 four hour shifts with no driving of company vehicles involved. However, within a couple of months the employer told him he would have to return to a 39 hour week, or he would lose his job.

In January, 2011 the employee was absent from work on sick leave as his doctor said he could only do 20 hours per week. This impacted on the employee negatively, as he was used to going to work full time since 1965.

The employer arranged an independent medical assessment in June, 2011 and in August, 2011, and the claimant was dismissed because the employer could not give him 20 hours per week only, and the employee was not able to work 39 hours.

The employee appealed this decision internally, but was unsuccessful.

He then brought a claim to the Equality Tribunal that he was discriminated against on the grounds of his disability-the brain tumour-and also that the employer failed, contrary to S. 16 of the Employment Equality Acts to provide "reasonable accommodation" for his return to work.

Decision of the Equality Tribunal

Firstly, the Tribunal decided that the long term illness arising from the brain tumour, even when treated successfully, was a "disability" within the terms of the Employment Equality Acts.

The employee pointed out to the employer that, as he was only being paid for the 20 hours worked and overtime was cut, it was in the employer's interest, and was not actually costing the employer disproportionately to permit him to work 20 hours per week.

He also offered to share the job with his son, who was also employed by the quarry, with his son doing the balance of the 39 hours.

The employee was 62 and only had 3 years to go to retirement, and rang the employer regularly asking to be accommodated with the 20 hours work week. His position was that allowing him to do so did not place a disproportionate burden on the employer, but the employer did not engage with him in a meaningful way in trying to accommodate a return to work.

The employer said that it needed the machine operated by the employee to be operated in a full time capacity.

However, it did not comment at the hearing on the offer of the man's son sharing the job to ensure this happened.

The employer also referred to a department of Social Welfare scheme, which allowed the employer to accommodate the employee in the first instance. The Department of Social Protection facilitated this by allowing workers to earn wages in their jobs without affecting their entitlement to illness benefit. However, this scheme came to an end, and it was then that the employer decided that it was 39 hours per week or dismissal.

The Tribunal found that regardless of any support provided by the Department of Social Welfare in these circumstances, the employer still had an obligation under the Employment Equality Acts to try to accommodate the employee.

The tribunal also found that permitting part-time work is one way in which reasonable accommodation can be provided, and that the employer failed to provide reasonable accommodation to the employee within section 16 of the Employment Equality Acts, and the worker was entitled to succeed in this aspect of his claim.

His complaint of discriminatory dismissal was also upheld as the Tribunal found that his dismissal was directly related to his disability, and to the employer's failure to provide reasonable accommodation to him to return to work.

The Tribunal awarded him the maximum amount it could award in this case-€40,000- and noted that this was compensation, not pay, and was therefore not subject to tax.

Lesson

This case saw the complainant making a written submission to the Equality Tribunal, but the Receiver of the respondent employer-to which a Receiver had been appointed-did not. It would be difficult to envisage circumstances in any of these cases where it would not be advisable to make a written submission to whoever is the deciding body.

A claim such as this one also requires the complainant, in the first instance, to establish a prima facie case. If he can do so, then the burden of proof shifts to the respondent to prove that he did not discriminate against the worker.

"In evaluating the evidence before me, I must first consider whether the complainant has established a prima facie case pursuant to S. 85A of the Acts."

This case also saw the respondent making an initial effort to accommodate the complainant in a return to work, but a decision was then taken to dismiss. This decision was taken within two days of receipt of the complainant's doctor's report stating that he was not fit to do full time work, and had a poor tolerance of sound.

The employer must make "reasonable accommodation" to facilitate the return of a worker to employment where he suffers from a disability. The employer needs to make a greater effort than occurred in this case, provided there is not a disproportionate burden placed on the employer from a resources or financial perspective.

Read the full decision here:
http://www.workplacerelations.ie/en/Cases/2014/September/DEC-E2014-066.html

Termination of Employment on Grounds of Incapacity-2 Vitally Important Long Term Sick Leave Cases

Long term sick leave.

Many employers have to deal with employees absent from work on long term sick leave, and are unsure of how to handle them. Two cases which should be studied closely for guidance in this area are:

An Equality Tribunal case (E2011-114), Eugena Carroll and H.J. Heinz Frozen & Chilled Foods Limited and

An Employment Appeals Tribunal case, *De Sousa v Kepak Group, UD964/2011*.

Let's take a look at *De Sousa v Kepak Group, UD964/2011* first. Bear in mind that this case is not strictly a "discrimination" case, as it was not brought to the Equality Tribunal, but it is similar to the Eugena Carroll case, which was brought on discriminatory grounds.

DE SOUSA V KEPAK GROUP

Mr. De Sousa was employed as a butcher with the Kepak Group from 2002. He suffered back pain in work in 2004 and in 2007, despite attending a physiotherapist for his back pain, was unable to attend work due to ongoing back pain.

He returned to work in March, 2008 but had to stop again in June, 2008. He returned again in 2009 but only lasted 1 day and had to quit again.

He was certified fit to return to work in October, 2010, but complained of back pain and collapsed resulting in an ambulance being called.

In November, 2010 the Site Manager wrote to him and told him that due to his absence from, and unavailability for, work the contract of employment between them was frustrated and dismissed him.

Mr. De Sosa brought a claim for unfair dismissal.

EAT Decision
The EAT found that Mr. De Sosa stayed in contact with the employer during his illness, and the employer was anxious to retain Mr. De Sosa in employment.

However, there were no jobs in the Kepak plant that were suitable for Mr. De Sosa, as administrative jobs had become computerised, and other work such as sweeping the floor involved some physical activity.

The employee was assisted in his return to work, being given the least demanding physical job available, as a trimmer. However, when this did not work out, the employer wrote to him telling him that his employment was under review due to his inability to perform the contract.

The letter of termination gave Mr. De Sosa an opportunity to appeal the decision, which he did not avail of.

The EAT found that the *Unfair Dismissals act 1977* had no application in this case, as the contract of employment was terminated by operation of law, as the contract had become inoperable and was frustrated.

Read the full case here: http://employmentrightsireland.com/wp-content/uploads/2014/10/de-sousa-v-kepak.pdf

Eugena Carroll and H.J. Heinz Frozen & Chilled Foods Limited

This case involved a dismissal where the employee claimed that she was discriminated against as a result of her disability, and reasonable accommodation was not made for her return to work. She brought her claim for discrimination on gender and disability grounds under the Employment Equality Acts.

Ms. Carroll was employed as a general operative by H.J. Heinz Frozen & Chilled Foods Limited on the 12th July, 1993, and she was dismissed on the 15th June, 2007.

She initially worked in the bakery department, but after it was closed she was transferred to clerical work in the purchasing area.

She was not happy there because she had no training for the work assigned to her. She then moved to engineering stores doing stocktaking, and later was transferred to the chilled food department. At first, she worked on the frozen food line which involved lifting up to 25kgs. She then moved to the production line which involved putting food into trays.

She went out sick from work at the end of March 2004, with repetitive strain injury, and was referred for physiotherapy. Unfortunately, her condition did not improve and she was referred to a consultant, and it was diagnosed she was also suffering from fibromyalgia.

She was seen by the company's occupational health advisor on a number of occasions. The complainant's medical advice, which the company had been kept fully informed about, was that she could not work in a cold environment such as that which obtained in the chilled department, and that she could not lift heavy weights.

She said that she was anxious to go back to work, and she believed that the company could have found work for her in the non chilled area, or in the clerical area.

She said that she had several meetings with Occupational Health and with HR, but no suitable position was offered to her, other than to return to the chilled area, or in an area where she was required to lift weights which she could not do because of her medical condition.

She said that she wanted to return to work, but could not give a return date because she was not fit to return to the position in the chilled area. She was called to a meeting with her manager and HR on the 15th of June, 2007, and because she was not able to give them a return to work date, and there were no alternative positions in the company which could accommodate the restrictions, she was informed, given that she was on sick leave for over 3 years that the company had decided to terminate her employment.

She was advised of her right to appeal. Her appeal was unsuccessful.

The complainant submitted to the Equality Tribunal that the dismissal was discriminatory, in that she was not offered reasonable accommodation because of her disability.

Decision of the Equality Officer
The 1st thing the employee has to do in a case like this is to establish a "prima facie" case of discrimination. This decision of the Equality Tribunal is worth close study and consideration, because it sets out a

template for how to deal with a termination on the basis of incapacity and frustration of the contract. For this reason, I have quoted extensively from the Equality Tribunal deciding officer.

The Equality Officer held:

"I am satisfied that the complainant's condition is a disability within the meaning of the Acts. Having heard the evidence I am satisfied that the complainant was dismissed from the employment for reasons connected with her capacity to perform her job due to her disability. Therefore she has established a prima facie case of discriminatory dismissal."

"In considering this case I am guided by the Labour Court determination in the case of Humphrey's v Westwood Fitness Club Det. No. EED037 and which was upheld by the Circuit Court. The case concerned a complaint of dismissal on the disability ground and whether the defence under section 16(1)(b) of the Acts was applicable. The Labour Court set out the test which should be applied to by an employer if they have formed a bona fide belief that the complainant is no longer able to perform the duties for which they are employed and stated:

At a minimum, however, an employer, should ensure that he or she in full possession of all the material facts concerning the employee's condition and that the employee is given fair notice that the question of his or her dismissal for incapacity is being considered. The employee must also be allowed an opportunity to influence the employer's decision.

In practical terms this will normally require a two-stage enquiry, which looks firstly at the factual position concerning the employee's capability including the degree of impairment arising from the disability and its likely duration. This would involve looking at the medical evidence available to the employer either from the employee's doctors or obtained independently.

Secondly, if it is apparent that the employee is not fully capable Section 16(3) of the Act requires the employer to consider what if any special treatment or facilities may be available by which the employee can become fully capable. The Section requires that the cost of such special treatment or facilities must also be considered. Here, what constitutes nominal cost will depend on the size of the organisation and its financial resources.

Finally, such an enquiry could only be regarded as adequate if the employee concerned is allowed a full opportunity to participate at each level and is allowed to present relevant medical evidence and submissions."

Dunne J. in the Circuit Court stated that the "there is a legal obligation under the Employment Equality Acts for an employer to take advice from either the complainant's own doctor, or an independent doctor, where there are concerns in relations to the health of a worker."

"In relation to the first part of the test which requires the respondent to obtain facts about the complainant's medical condition, I note that the respondent had several medical reports about the complainant's medical condition both from her GP and the company's own doctor and these medical reports stated that she could not work in temperatures below 18 to 20 degrees or lift weights in excess of one or two kilogram's. I note also that the respondent called the complainant to a number of meetings with the company where the option of returning to work in the light of her medical condition was discussed. I am satisfied that the respondent appraised himself of the full facts about the medical condition, through reports from the complainant's GP and the company's own doctor, before making a decision to dismiss her. I am also satisfied that the respondent gave the complainant notice that he was considering her dismissal due to her incapacity."

"In relation to the second leg of the above test which relates to reasonable accommodation, I have examined the evidence and I note that the respondent made several suggestions about the complainant returning to work in the chilled department but her medical condition prevented her working there as all the operator roles were below 10 degrees and she required a temperature of between 18 and 20 degrees."

"The company offered her subject to medical certification to bring her back to work on a three day week, light duties and a rotational position but the complainant's GP would not certify her fit to return to the positions offered because of the temperature restrictions. I note that the respondent e-mailed all the heads of department on four occasions over the three year period of the complainant's sick leave seeking alternative roles but there were no suitable vacancies except in the production area were available. Likewise I note that the complainant was also asked to do a virtual tour of the company with OH to identify roles which were suitable for her. A number of roles were deemed suitable and she was advised that the position would only be available if a vacancy existed. There were a number of vacancies in these areas over this period but the complainant did not have the qualifications or experience required."

"I am satisfied that the dismissal of the complainant was due to her incapacity because of her disability to perform the work she was employed to do and in the circumstances the dismissal was not a discriminatory dismissal. Having regard to the provisions of Section 16(1)(b), I find that the dismissal was lawful in accordance with that provision."

"I find that:

the respondent did not discriminate against the complainant on the disability grounds pursuant to section 6(2)(g) of the Acts and contrary to section 8(6) of the Acts in relation to her dismissal and that the defence under Section 16(1)(b) applied;

(ii) the respondent did not discriminate against the complainant on the disability ground pursuant to section 6(2)(g) of the Acts in relation to the provision of reasonable accommodation to the complainant in accordance with section 16(3)(b) of the Acts."

Lesson

If the employer is considering terminating the contract of employment on the grounds of incapacity, there is a 2 step test to be carried out:

1) the employer must be in possession of all the facts concerning the employee's condition, and the employee must be told that the question of dismissal is being considered on the grounds of incapacity. This would involve looking at the medical evidence, either from the employee's doctor or obtained independently.

2) if the employee is not fully capable, can he be accommodated by the use of special treatment or facilities to become fully capable? The employer must make "reasonable accommodation" to allow the employee return to work.

If an employer was to follow the steps taken by the employer in the Carroll v Heinz foods case above, he should be in a strong position to defend a dismissal on the grounds of incapacity.

Read the full Carroll v Heinz foods case here:
http://www.workplacerelations.ie/en/Cases/2011/June/DEC-E2011-114-Full-Case-Report.html

3. Temporary Agency Workers

Forklift Driver Wins Over €20,000 Under New Temporary Agency Work Legislation

The *Protection of Employees (Temporary Agency Work) Act, 2012* came into effect in May, 2012 and offers additional protection to agency workers. It is notable that the pay provisions of the act were made retrospective to December, 2011.

This case-*Team Obair Limited and Robert Costello*-involved a fork lift driver who was paid €13.50 per hour. He first brought his case to the Rights Commissioner service and failed. He then brought this appeal to the Labour Court.

He was arguing that he should have been paid the going rate for forklift drivers at the hirer's workplace in accordance with s.6(1) of the Act.

The hirer in this case was Logistics Company Shannon Transport Logistics (STL), who had the contract to provide services to Diageo Guinness Ireland. Diageo traditionally paid €18.50 per hour to forklift drivers.

The Claimant was employed at a plant operated by Diageo Guinness Ireland Limited at St James Gate Dublin. The work in which he was engaged was historically undertaken by workers directly employed by Diageo. As a result of restructuring by Diageo Guinness Ireland Limited, this work was contracted out to third party undertakings during the 1990s. The contracts for the provision of this service were awarded by way of tender. Various third parties were awarded the contract through this process in the intervening years.

Team Obair Limited was contracted to provide agency workers to the original third party contractors and on each occasion on which the contract passed from one contractor to another the Respondent retained the business of providing agency workers to the incoming contractor.

Team Obair Limited, an employment agency and this man's employer, told the Court that when it commenced the contract it obtained a statement in writing from Logistics Company Shannon Transport Logistics (STL), to whom the man was assigned. This was pursuant to s.15 of the Act, and set out the basic terms and conditions that it would apply if it employed workers directly on the same work as that undertaken by agency workers assigned to it by the Respondent.

In that statement the hirer indicated that it would pay forklift workers the same rate as that paid to the Claimant by the Respondent, that is, €13.50 per hour.

This case really turned on the argument by the Respondent (Team Obair Limited) that the forklift driver rates of €18.50 were historical and would not be paid now if taking on drivers.

The Court stated:

"In this case the rates paid by the hirer are not formally prescribed in a collective agreement. According to the Union (SIPTU) they are determined by an arrangement established by custom and practice whereby rates are carried forward and modified from time to time by collective bargaining. The Respondent did not take issue with the Union's contention in that regard.

Unlike other similar employment rights statutes the Act does not require a claim for equal pay to be grounded by reference to an actual comparator. Nevertheless, the rate that is paid to employees of the hirer who are engaged in the same type of work is an important evidential tool.

While this is acknowledged by the Respondent it contended that those rates are historical. It submitted that if the hirer took on new employees at the time that the Claimant's assignment is deemed to have commenced the rates payable would be those specified in the s.15 notification upon which it relies. That, however, is a mere assertion which cannot be elevated to an evidential basis upon which the Court could make findings of fact. In particular, the Respondent has not pointed to any pay determination arrangement operated by the hirer the application of which might result in fork lift drivers being paid €13.50 per hour.

However, the Court found that this argument, if accepted, would be "subversive to the purpose of the legislation and render it nugatory".

The Court found:

"For these reasons, and in the absence of any reliable evidence to the contrary, the Court has come to the conclusion that it is more probable than not that had the Claimant been employed by the hirer on 5th December 2011 he would have been paid €18.50 in line with other fork lift drivers similarly employed. Accordingly, that is the rate to which he is entitled pursuant to s.6(1) of the Act. Accordingly the Court must hold that the Claimant is entitled to succeed in this appeal."

It then ordered:

"In accordance with Clauses (a) and (b) of sub paragraph (3) above, the Court declares that the Claimant's complaint is well founded and it directs the Respondent herein to adjust the Claimant's rate of pay to €740 per 40 hour week, or €18.50 per hour, with effect from 5th December 2011."

This worked out at in excess of €200 per week with effect from December, 2011 and the decision was handed down in November, 2013.

Lesson

Agency workers enjoy a much greater degree of protection thanks to the Protection of Employees (Temporary Agency Work) Act, 2012, and is is likely that there will be more cases along the lines of this one.

It is worth noting that it is possible for an employment agency to be indemnified against losses arising from claims, because of inaccurate informant provided by the hirer.

Section 15 of the Protection of Employees (Temporary Agency Work) Act 2012 states:

15.— (1) It shall be the duty of the hirer of an agency worker to provide the employment agency that employs that agency worker with all such information in the possession of the hirer as the employment agency reasonably requires to enable the employment agency to comply with its obligations under this Act in relation to the agency worker.

(2) Where proceedings in respect of a contravention of this Act are brought by an agency worker against an employment agency and the contravention is attributable to the failure by the hirer of the agency worker to comply with this section, the hirer shall indemnify the employment agency in respect of any loss incurred by the employment agency that is attributable to such failure.

Read the full decision here:
http://www.workplacerelations.ie/en/Cases/2013/November/AWD134.html

4. TRANSFER OF UNDERTAKINGS (TUPE)

STATIC GUARD AWARDED €11,500 UNDER TUPE (PROTECTION OF EMPLOYEES ON TRANSFER OF UNDERTAKINGS) REGULATIONS

Tupe regulations can be incredibly difficult to fully understand, and is a complex area of employment law.

This case was a 2013 decision, and involved the transfer of an undertaking in 2011 where the static guard transferred from one employer to another, and the claim was brought under *European Communities (Protection of Employees on Transfer of Undertakings) Regulations, 2003.*

This employee was a static guard at business centre in Limerick, and he transferred employment following the transfer of an undertaking. Prior to the transfer he worked 47.5 hours per week, starting at 8.30 am and finishing at 6 pm; after the transfer he was asked to start at 8.00 am as the employer had contracted to provide 50 hours per week to the business center.

This meant he was then working 50 hours per week, in contravention of Organisation of Working Time Act,1997, which caused concern to the general manager of the new employer.

His hours were then reduced to 48 hours per week with immediate effect.

The employer claimed, in an effort to reduce costs, that a national agreement with SIPTU re static guards had been arrived at involving putting static guards on an averaging arrangement where they worked 48/36 hours alternately, giving them an average of 42 hours per week.

The employee claimed there was no national agreement, and he did not want to work on other sites as this would have involved working nights.

The employee was then given a further notice of reduction in hours to 40 hours per week, which amounted to 4 days' work rather than 5.

The employer claimed there was no sense in giving 5 days' work resulting in a 47.5 hour week, as the normal working day in the centre was 10 hours. This would have involved giving 2.5 hours per week to another employee.

The Employment Appeals Tribunal found no documentary evidence of a national agreement, and that the employee was entitled to stay on a 47.5 hour week, as he had enjoyed prior to transfer.

The Tribunal varied the decision of Rights Commissioner and awarded €11,500 under European Communities (Protection of Employees on Transfer of Undertakings) Regulations 2003 to the employee.

It stated:

"The Tribunal is satisfied that claim is well founded and the employee had an entitlement to remain on the 47.5 hours per week which he was working prior to the transfer. Nevertheless, as the centre, at which the employee wished and was entitled to remain, operated on a ten-hour five-day week basis, which hours exceeded the maximum permissible under the Organisation of Working Time Act, and it being impractical to provide another employee for 2.5 hours a week, the Tribunal finds it just and equitable in all the circumstance to vary the decision of the Rights Commissioner and awards the employee €11,500-00 under the European Communities (Protection of Employees on Transfer of Undertakings) Regulations, 2003."

Lesson

The EAT recognised the worker's right to enjoy the same terms and conditions after the transfer of employment under the TUPE regulations. However, it also recognised that it would have been impractical to enforce this as it would have resulted in the employer having to employ someone for 2.5 hours per week, or accept the employee working the maximum permissible hours under the *Organisation of Working Time Act, 1997*. Accordingly it awarded the employee the monetary sum of €11,500 in compensation.

Read the full decision here: http://employmentlawireland.ie/wp-content/uploads/2013/08/tupe-transfer-of-undertaking.pdf

5. Unfair Dismissals

Montessori Teacher Awarded €32,500 for Unfair Dismissal in Kildare

This case involved a Montessori school in Kildare and the dismissal of the Principal of the school.

A Board of Trustees ran the school. The Principal went on administrative leave in 2010, following a complaint from a parent that the Montessori method was not being used by the Principal in her class.

The Vice Principal took over the Principal's class and the Board asked Vice Principal for a report on each child.

The Principal was very unhappy with this report, as she felt the Vice Principal was trying to undermine her position. The report also questioned the Principal's competence, professionalism, and commitment to the school's method.

The Principal alleged the report was defamatory and offensive, and wrote to the Board with her views.

She also gave a copy of the letter to the Vice Principal, and asked her to reflect on her report and consider her position.

The Principal was then invited to a disciplinary hearing, the purpose of which was to discuss the Principal's actions/behaviour towards Vice Principal.

The Principal allegedly had asked the Board to remove Vice Principal from school, although later the Principal claimed she only wanted the Vice Principal removed from the acting Principal post.

The Board sought advice from a HR consultant and initiated a disciplinary process.

At the disciplinary hearing, the Principal clarified that she only wanted the Vice Principal removed from post of Vice Principal, not from her teaching post in the school.

A performance improvement weekly plan was initiated for the Principal.

However, the Board then decided that the Principal's action in handing a copy of her letter to the Board to the Vice Principal and asking Vice Principal to step down to be serious misconduct, and the Board decided termination of the Principal's employment was justified.

There were previous warnings on the Principal's file but these were not considered in arriving at the decision to dismiss.

The Principal was offered a right to appeal, which she did not take.

The Principal had suggested an independent facilitator to assist with the matter, and had no faith in the appeal's process.

She gave an independent facilitator background information to the dispute. The facilitator contacted the Board about the matter but the Principal was then suspended for a breach of the data protection laws and policy of the school.

The Principal attended the disciplinary hearing with her solicitor, and stated that she felt her position was undermined by the Vice Principal's report while the Principal was on administrative leave. She also said she saw no point in questioning Vice Principal at the disciplinary hearing.

The Principal was dismissed on 3rd March, 2011.

The Employment Appeals Tribunal found that the procedures used by the Board were unsatisfactory, while it would have been helpful if principal availed of the appeal process. However, it recognised that she was not obliged to do so.

Nevertheless, the Employment Appeals Tribunal found that the Principal was unfairly dismissed and awarded €32,500 compensation.

Lesson

This case is yet another example of the most common reason for a successful unfair dismissal claim: failure to follow fair procedures and/or ensure that the employee's constitutional right to fair play and natural justice is upheld and respected. Many employers fail to recognise that, regardless of the particular facts of a case, if an employee is not afforded fair procedures the facts may be of little or any significance in the ultimate decision of the EAT, or any other body deciding the case.

Read the full case here: http://educationlawireland.com/wp-content/uploads/2013/07/montessori-teacher-unfair-dismissal.pdf

Unfair Selection for Redundancy-Awarded €50,000 for Unfair Dismissal

This case involved the unfair selection for redundancy of a Regional Environmental Manager in a waste/environmental company, Oxigen Environmental. In the grounds of claim, it was stated that the claimant had commenced in the role of Environmental Compliance Officer, but that the role had evolved through promotion to include, at various times, management of Civic Amenity Sites, Contract and Site Management, Facility Manager for Ballymount, transport co-ordination, environmental management on all Dublin sites and the Midlands Region and commercial tendering.

On 29 April 2010, during the course of a meeting with the General Manager and the Human Resource Manager, the claimant was informed that the Compliance structure in the business was being flattened and that her role would cease to exist.

The company had only decided a week earlier that her role would cease. The claimant said she was unfairly dismissed and sought reinstatement; alternatively, she claimed that she was unfairly selected for redundancy.

The company claimed that her redundancy was part of a company restructuring, and that she had been informed of her potential redundancy on 29th April, 2010.

The redundancy was confirmed on 26th May, 2010, and came into effect on 26th June, 2010.

The claimant was the only person who worked in the role of Regional Environment Manager and, following her departure, the role ceased to exist.

The claimant did not appeal.

However, in its decision the EAT stated:

"The fact that the claimant did not appeal the dismissal was considered by the Tribunal but the Tribunal notes that the appeal would have to be made to SD, the chairman of the Company. The Tribunal further notes that SD was at the meeting which took the decision to dismiss the claimant. Therefore, it would be entirely inappropriate, and contrary to fair procedures, that he should hear the appeal.

The Employment Appeals Tribunal found that claimant was not treated fairly or reasonably, and commented that the selection criteria must be objectively applied in a fair manner; it stated that there was no hard and fast rules for deciding the criteria to be used.

But the criteria will come under close scrutiny if the employee claims he/she was unfairly selected."

It stated:

"When an employer is making an employee redundant, while retaining other employees, the selection criteria being used should be objectively applied in a fair manner. While there are no hard and fast rules as to what constitutes the criteria to be adopted nevertheless the criteria adopted will come under close scrutiny if an employee claims that he/she was unfairly selected for redundancy. The employer must follow the agreed procedure when making the selection.

Where there is no agreed procedure in relation to selection for redundancy, as in this case, then the employer must act fairly and reasonably.

The Tribunal noted that the respondent kept taking away parts of the claimant's job and that interviewing had taken place on 12 May 2010 for an alternative position within the company for which a job specification was not formulated until 14 May 2010. The Tribunal finds this most surprising. The Tribunal also takes the view that the claimant could have done a health-and-safety manager job which ultimately took on a construction-related title given that she had no construction-related qualification. The respondent had tried to row back and disadvantage the claimant.

The Tribunal does not accept that the Respondent acted fairly and reasonably in this case for the following reasons:

1. the decision to make the claimant redundant was taken at a meeting in a hotel in County Louth on the 23rd April 2010. The chairman of the company (SD) attended this meeting;

2. there was no serious or worthwhile consultation with the claimant prior to making her redundant. The consultation should be real and substantial. The decision to make the claimant's position redundant was taken before the consultation process commenced;

3. no suitable or substantial consideration was given to alternatives to dismissing the claimant by reason of redundancy;

4. there was no worthwhile discussion in relation to the criteria used for selecting the claimant. The selection criteria should apply to all employees working in the same area as the claimant but should also consider other positions which the claimant is capable of doing."

Employers must act reasonably in taking a decision to dismiss an employee on the grounds of redundancy. Indeed, *Section 5 of the Unfair Dismissals (Amendment) Act, 1993*, provides that the reasonableness of the employer's conduct is now an essential factor to be considered in the context of all dismissals. Section 5, inter alia, stipulates that: "…..in determining if a dismissal is an unfair dismissal, regard may be had……to the reasonableness or otherwise of the conduct (whether by act or omission) of the employer in relation to the dismissal"

The EA Tribunal found, therefore, that the claimant was unfairly dismissed by virtue of her unfair selection for redundancy, and awarded €50,000 euro for unfair dismissal in addition to the redundancy payment of €10,014 already paid to the claimant under Redundancy Payments acts 1967-2007.

Lesson

The EAT appeared to be skeptical about the employer's actions in this case, and you will see from the Tribunal's comments in its decision that it will look closely at the steps taken by the employer in carrying out a redundancy. Employers can be tempted to dress up a dismissal as a redundancy in getting rid of an employee that they may consider troublesome or difficult. However, the employer needs to be very aware that his actions will be scrutinised closely afterwards, if there is a claim.

Read the full decision here: http://employmentlawireland.ie/wp-content/uploads/2013/07/unfair-selection-for-redundancy-oxigen.pdf

Creche Worker's Week Cut from 5 Days to 3-Wins €10,000 for Constructive Dismissal

This case involved a crèche worker (child minder) whose working week was cut from 5 days to 3 due to the financial pressure on the employer. She was awarded €10,000 for constructive dismissal.

The employee was a creche worker since 2006, and she left her employment in 2010. She had been on the same wage, €404, throughout her employment.

The employer wanted to introduce a 10% pay cut, but the employee refused to sign the letter consenting to the wage cut. The employee also noted that she was as busy as she ever was, and had to regularly work unpaid hours during the week.

The claimant explained to the owners of the creche that she did not think it was reasonable to take a pay cut after five years without an increase, and that she worked extra hours without recompense. She was asked to sign the agreement form by Monday or she would not have a job. She asked if he meant she would be dismissed, and he said no but the crèche would have to close.

The claimant's working week was cut to 3 days from 5 days, effectively a 40% reduction in her pay. However, her contract stated *"normal working week will be 5 days, Monday to Friday"*.

She met the Manager when she arrived to the creche and asked for the change to her shifts to be put in writing. The Manager refused, so she asked for a witness to be present to hear the Manager say she was not required on Monday or Tuesday. The chef came to the meeting. The Manager said that the claimant was not required that day or the next, and that the claimant had refused to leave the building when asked. The Manager then asked the claimant to leave. The claimant left and went to her GP.

The employee was certified unfit to work by her doctor, but she eventually resigned and did not invoke the grievance procedure in the workplace.

The Employment Appeals Tribunal applied its usual tests in a case of constructive dismissal and looked at whether there was a *"significant breach of the employment contract"*.

"The burden of proof, which is a very high one, lies with the claimant. She must show that her resignation was not voluntary. The legal test to be applied is "an and or test" . Firstly, the Tribunal must look at the contract of employment and establish whether or not there has been a significant breach going to the root of the contract. If the Tribunal is not satisfied that there has been a significant breach of the contract it can examine the conduct of both the employee and employer together with all the circumstances surrounding the termination to establish whether or not the decision of the employee to termination the contract was a reasonable one.

The claimant made her claim for constructive dismissal under the following heading:

Unilateral alteration of her contractual terms (cut of her working week from five days to three days.)

It found that "employee was singled out following refusal to sign letter" and that the employer then unilaterally altered the terms and conditions of the employment contract by reducing the working week from 5 days to 3."

The legal test the claimant must satisfy is an onerous one. Firstly, the claimant must show that there has been a significant breach going to the root of the contract, which said breach prevented the claimant from carrying out her contractual duties. It is very clear from the evidence that the claimant was singled out following her refusal to sign the letter of consent.

The respondent's counsel even put it to her that because she had refused to give her consent she had placed herself in a better position that those who had signed it and therefore the respondent had to treat her differently and find another way to make the cuts. Following her refusal to sign the consent the respondent attempted to unilaterally alter the terms of her contract by reducing her working days from five to three and thus reducing her remuneration by 40%. That is a breach of her contract. It is a breach that goes to the root of her contract. It is a breach which prevented her from carrying out her contractual duties.

The Tribunal found that the claimant was constructively dismissed and awarded her €10,000 in compensation.

LESSON

The critical lesson here is the test applied by the EAT in assessing whether an employee has been constructively dismissed or not, recognising as it does that the burden of proof is on the employee and is an onerous one.

The EAT was satisfied that there was a unilateral breach of her contract:

Following her refusal to sign the consent the respondent attempted to unilaterally alter the terms of her contract by reducing her working days from five to three and thus reducing her remuneration by 40%. That is a breach of her contract. It is a breach that goes to the root of her contract. It is a breach which prevented her from carrying out her contractual duties.

Any employee considering bringing a claim for constructive dismissal should not underestimate the difficulty in passing the test which the EAT employs. Interestingly, in this case the employee did not invoke the internal grievance procedure. This would normally be strongly recommended if an employee was considering ultimately bringing a claim for constructive dismissal.

Read the full case here: http://employmentlawireland.ie/wp-content/uploads/2013/07/creche-worker-constructive-dismissal.pdf

Unfair Selection of Warehouse Operative for Redundancy-Awarded Compensation of €8,000

This case involved a warehouse operative, working in Waterford for a kitchen seller, who was made redundant.

He was awarded €8,000 for 'completely deficient procedures' in implementing redundancy.

The employer company sold kitchens throughout the country, and the claimant worked as a warehouse operative in the Waterford branch.

There were poor sales in the Waterford branch, and the claimant's position was selected for redundancy.

The company invited applications for voluntary redundancy or career break, and the claimant was offered a position in Limerick but he declined this for 'family reasons'.

He signed the RP50 form and accepted the redundancy cheque.

He was advised of his right to appeal.

The General Manager claimed company policy re redundancy was adhered to, and there was no need to compile a redundancy matrix as warehouse was closing fully.

Another employee was retained to complete an order.

However, at the EAT hearing there was no evidence of financial figures for the Waterford branch.

It was the claimant's evidence that there were times when he was involved in heated debates with the branch manager. The claimant received one verbal warning following the invoking of the disciplinary procedures for an error he made.

He also felt there was a personal issue between himself and the Branch Manager, and that she did not want him working in the branch.

When the claimant's position was made redundant he understood that the warehouse was shutting fully, and that any future orders would be sent from another branch. However, the claimant stated that to the best of his knowledge, the warehouse did not in fact close immediately and that there were still employees working in the warehouse at the time of his claim, as the employees from the trade counter also worked in the warehouse section. The claimant could not understand how employees with lesser service were retained, as he could have been trained in most of the positions.

Decision

The Employment Appeals Tribunal accepted that company was suffering losses; however, the procedures for the claimant's dismissal were *'completely deficient'* and awarded €8,000 compensation under Unfair Dismissals Acts, 1977 to 2007 with the redundancy sum already paid to be offset against the €8,000.

Lesson

This case demonstrates once again the need for an employer to afford fair play and good procedures in dealing with employees, regardless of whether it is a dismissal, or redundancy situation. The EAT accepted the company's assertion that it was suffering losses, but noted that there was no supporting documentation for this. Clearly, this could not have helped the employer's case when it came before the tribunal.

There was also a preliminary issue raised by the employer that the EAT did not have jurisdiction to hear the claim as the employee did not sign the T1A form; rather, it was his representative who signed it.

However the EAT decided that it did have jurisdiction as the form could be signed by the employee's representative.

Read the full decision here: http://employmentlawireland.ie/wp-content/uploads/2013/06/unfair-selection-for-redundancy.pdf

Abrekbabra Supervisor Awarded €9,500 For Unfair Dismissal-'Forgot to Pay' for Food

In this case, an Abrekebabra fast food restaurant supervisor, accused of consuming food on the premises without any record of the food having been purchased, won an award of €9,500 for unfair dismissal.

The background is that he was a supervisor since 2006, and was given a number of verbal warnings for breach of company rules, with final written warning being issued in April, 2010.

The CCTV footage showed him consuming food with no record of payment. The supervisor claimed he *'forgot to'*, but management went back over other CCTV footage and noticed other alleged instances of food being consumed and not being paid for.

The employee attempted to pay next day, but the employer was not happy, viewing it as a breach of trust and gave the employee one month's notice and dismissed him.

However, the employer gave no letter to claimant confirming the dismissal, and did not give him the opportunity to appeal.

The supervisor denied receiving verbal warnings, but he agreed he had received a written warning. The Tribunal found a direct conflict of evidence between parties, and also a *'lack of proper procedures'* in effecting dismissal-there was no formal invitation to dismissal meeting, no investigation, no letter to claimant confirming dismissal, no opportunity to appeal, and he did not receive his full notice entitlement.

The tribunal found he was unfairly dismissed, and awarded him €9,500.

Lesson

The question of fair procedures and natural justice is the key to this case and the win for the employee. The facts alleged as to non payment for food, and so on, are irrelevant, to a great extent, when the employer fails to give the employee fair play, and the opportunity to defend himself, and the chance to appeal an adverse outcome/decision.

Read the full decision here: http://employmentlawireland.ie/wp-content/uploads/2013/06/abrakebabra.pdf

Mechanic Fails in Constructive Dismissal Claim-Burden of Proof 'Very High'

This case involved a mechanic who left work because of 'work related stress' and brought a claim for constructive dismissal.

The EAT reaffirmed that the *'burden of proof is very high'* in constructive dismissal cases.

This is so, because the burden of proof is on the employee to prove that she had no other option but to resign due to the unreasonableness of the employer.

In this case the mechanic, who had gone on sick leave in May, 2010, did not return to work and resigned from his position in September, 2010.

He then brought a case for constructive dismissal.

Decision of EAT

The Employment Appeals Tribunal in its decision referred to the burden of proof on the employee as being a *'very high one'*. It held that the employee must prove that his resignation was not voluntary.

It noted the definition of constructive dismissal:

Section 1 of the Unfair Dismissal Act defines constructive dismissal as:

" the termination by the employee of his contract of employment with this employer whether prior notice of the termination was or was not given to the employer in the circumstances in which, because of the conduct of the employer the employee was or would have been entitled or it was or would have been reasonable for the employee to terminate the contract of employment without giving prior notice of the termination to the employer."

The EAT went on to state:

"The burden of proof, which is a very high one, lies with the claimant. He must show that his resignation was not voluntary. The legal test to be applied is "an and or test". Firstly, the Tribunal must look at the contract of employment and establish whether or not there has been a significant breach going to the root of the contract. If the Tribunal is not satisfied that there has been a significant breach of the contract it can examine the conduct of both the employee and employer together with all the circumstances surrounding the termination to establish whether or not the decision of the employee to termination the contract was a reasonable one.

The EAT must look at the contract and decide whether there has been a significant breach of the employment contract going to the root of the contract.

If there has not been a breach by the employer, the EAT will then look at the conduct of the employer and employee, and decide on the 'reasonableness' of the decision of the employee to resign.

The claim by the claimant for constructive dismissal fell under three headings:

1. The excessive workload placed on him

2. Exclusion in the workplace, for example at lunch breaks

3. Being bullied and harassed in the workplace.

The claimant suffered from Asperger Syndrome.

He left work in May, 2010 and did not return due to stress, according to his parents and GP who stated it was work related.

However, the employer stated that he did not know this until he received a 2nd medical certificate.

The claimant stated that there was no contact with the employer after that. The employer stated that he did try to contact the claimant's father on several occasions.

The EAT held that it is crucial in a constructive dismissal case that the employee fully informs the employer of the complaints being made against him, and gives the employer the opportunity to resolve the problems."

Interestingly, the EAT in this case also held that the parents of the claimant had a duty to let the employer know of the issues.

In this unusual case, the claimant's parents had a duty to inform the employer why the claimant was suffering from stress and should have informed him that the claimant felt he was being subject to behaviour that amounted to bullying, harassment and exclusion. Their failure to do so left the employer powerless to rectify the situation.

The EAT found no significant breach of contract going to the root of the contract which would have prevented the employee from carrying out his duties as per the contract.

The EAT then examined the conduct of both parties and found that the decision of the employee to resign was not a reasonable one.

The claimant's claim failed with the EAT commenting that, whilst it had a great degree of sympathy for the claimant, it was bound to apply the law. It noted that the law made no allowance for someone suffering from Asperger Syndrome. (However this is not entirely true as the employment equality acts oblige employers to make "reasonable accommodation" for those suffering from a disability. Presumably what the EAT meant was that in applying the tests for constructive dismissal-breach of contract and/or reasonableness of the conduct of both parties-it could not consider the claimant's Asperger Syndrome).

LESSON

This case demonstrates again the difficulty in winning a case for constructive dismissal; the employee really must fully engage with the employer to have his issue resolved internally first. In this case, the claimant had no contact with the employer after leaving, and the Tribunal heard that the employer attempted to contact the claimant's father on several occasions, to no avail, in order to resolve the problems of the claimant.

Read the full decision here: http://employmentlawireland.ie/wp-content/uploads/2013/05/constructive-dismissal-ogorman-glen-tyre-company.pdf

Security Officer Denied Taking Money from Shopping Centre Pay Stations-Wins €46,800 for Unfair Dismissal

A security officer in a shopping centre, who denied misappropriating money from shopping centre pay stations, won his case for unfair dismissal and was awarded €46,800.

The claimant was a security officer employed by a property management company from 2004 to 2010.

His manager carried out an investigation into alleged misappropriation of funds, and the manager was satisfied that the findings merited referral onwards for possible disciplinary action.

He referred the case to a company director. The claimant categorically denied taking money.

However, the respondent went into liquidation and failed to appear to defend the claim.

The Employment Appeals Tribunal was not satisfied the claimant misappropriated the money, and the respondent did not prove the dismissal was fair.

The EAT therefore heard the uncontested evidence of the claimant in his claim for unfair dismissal, and awarded €46,800 and four weeks' pay under Minimum Notice and Terms of Employment Acts.

Lesson

The respondent went into liquidation in this case, and the employee's evidence was uncontested, which clearly made his case significantly easier. Nevertheless, the employee would have been anxious to restore his good name to continue working in the industry, even though the chances of being able to enforce his award were slim to non existent.

Read the full decision here: http://employmentlawireland.ie/wp-content/uploads/2013/04/2202-10-securiy-officer-ud1.pdf

UNFAIR SELECTION FOR REDUNDANCY CLAIM FAILS-€10,000 EX GRATIA PAYMENT OFFER REJECTED

The claimant in this case, an administrative training and development co-ordinator, brought a claim for unfair dismissal as a result of her redundancy. The basis of her claim was that she was unfairly selected for redundancy and the company could/should have given her alternative work, which she was willing to do.

The Employer was a large multi-national engineering company.

The claimant was responsible for administrative training, and had a development co-ordinator role lending support to apprentice electricians employed by the company. She also organised internal executive courses in leadership management and skills enhancement.

Due to the downturn in the construction industry, there was a large number of redundancies resulting in staff numbers reducing from a one time high of 500 down to 85.

The claimant was made redundant.

The number of apprentices reduced by over 90%, and the training and development courses for which the claimant had responsibility were outsourced to a university located in England.

The claimant's line manager was made redundant in March 2010, and the claimant's position was also made redundant in June 2010.

The company then advertised for 2 corporate human resource positions.

The positions were publicly advertised and carried a higher salary than that paid to the claimant. The company claimed that the claimant did not have requirements or experience for these positions.

The claimant was paid her statutory redundancy and one month's notice. She was also offered a €10,000 ex-gratia payment, which the claimant declined to accept.

She had received a massive shock at the meeting advising she was to be made redundant, and became emotional and did not speak.

She claimed that as she was not allowed to retrain or accept another role, she needed time to think about the ex gratia €10,000 offer. The employer would have required her to sign a waiver form which then never occurred.

The EAT had enormous sympathy for the claimant who it recognised as an excellent worker. However, it decide that this was a case of a genuine company restructuring and therefore a genuine redundancy.

It also held that there was no unfair selection for redundancy, and noted the respectful response by the company to cross examination of the claimant during the EAT hearing, and its offer of an ex gratia payment of €10,000, which it was not obliged to offer.

It held that the claimant was traumatised by redundancy and it may have affected her decision not to accept the ex gratia payment.

However the claim under the unfair dismissals acts failed and, as she received her statutory redundancy entitlement and received her correct notice of termination, her claim under the minimum notice and terms of employment acts claim failed also.

The Tribunal, however, is satisfied that a genuine restructuring was occurring within the respondent company due to significant economic changes which led to a redundancy situation.

The Tribunal is further satisfied on the evidence of both parties that the claimant's role became redundant and that there was no unfair selection of the claimant.

LESSON

This case can be contrasted with the case of the environmental manager at Oxigen Environmental, as the EAT in this case noted In all the circumstances, the respondent company acted reasonably and The respondent company did show sympathy for the claimant's loss by offering an ex-gratia payment of €10,000 to the claimant on her redundancy. This respectful response to the claimant's difficulties was further reflected in a similar approach to her cross-examination before the Tribunal by the respondent company's representative.

While there is no prescribed method of making a redundancy in a non collective redundancy situation, there is a requirement for the employer to act reasonably at all times in carrying out the redundancy.

Read the full decision here: http://employmentlawireland.ie/wp-content/uploads/2013/04/redundancy-unfair-selection-342-2011.pdf

FAS COMMUNITY EMPLOYMENT EMPLOYEE WINS UNFAIR DISMISSAL CASE AND IS REINSTATED

This case involved a FAS community employment scheme worker whose fixed term contract was not renewed. She brought a claim for unfair dismissal.

She was an employee with the Council as part of FAS Community Employment Scheme. She was employed on fixed term contracts from March, 2009 to October, 2009 and from October 2009 to October 2010-2 fixed term contracts.

The scheme ended and 11 people out of 12 on a list had their contract renewed.

The claimant's contract was not renewed, and it transpired at the hearing that she was dismissed on the recommendation of her line manager.

The EAT found that she was unfairly dismissed, and noted that there was two further years' work available which were not offered to the claimant. No reason was given to her, and she did not seek a reason on dismissal.

The Employment Appeals Tribunal directed her reinstatement for the remaining two years of work on the new scheme.

Lesson

The decision of unfair dismissal in this case appears to have been arrived at because no reason was given for the non renewal of the claimant's contract, in circumstances where there was a further 2 years work available. Remember: once a dismissal has taken place the burden is on the employer to show that it was not an unfair dismissal.

The Tribunal finds that the scheme supervisor gave the respondent no reason for such recommendation and the respondent sought none at the material time.

Accordingly the claim under the Unfair Dismissals Acts 1977-2007 succeeds and the Tribunal directs reinstatement of the claimant as and from 22 October 2010 for the remaining two years.

Read the full decision here: http://employmentlawireland.ie/wp-content/uploads/2013/04/fas-community-employment-scheme.pdf

Secondary School Secretary Awarded €9,850 for Unfair Dismissal

This case involved a secondary school secretary bringing a case for unfair dismissal, where the school's audit showed up a shortfall of approximately €12,000 in the school's finances.

The employer was a secondary school and the claimant was a full time secretary from March, 2007 until she went on leave of absence to Australia in October, 2008.

There was a number of versions of the employment contract but, in any event, the claimant's role was to, along with other administrative duties, record and lodge school income.

However, during the course of her employment the school's power supply was disconnected due to unpaid bills. There was also an unpaid newspaper bill, for which the school received embarrassing reminders.

The Principal became concerned about these unpaid bills, and stale cheques which had been made out to the school but not lodged.

The Principal issued a warning to the secretary, and the secretary was later granted leave of absence by the Chairperson of the Board of Management from October, 2008.

The claimant went to Australia; however an audit uncovered an 'unexplained and unaccountable absence of money' from the school accounts.

That audit, and ongoing calls from customers about payments, revealed, at first, shortcomings in settling invoices and bills, and later a sizeable unexplained and unaccountable absence of money. With the aid of photocopies of many lodgements, the principal indicated that the claimant recorded taking in money but a lot of it remained missing. This was brought to the attention of the school's accountant, and it was decided that the claimant needed to be spoken to about this. The Principal and accountant reacted, firstly with disbelief at the notion and amount of missing money, but that feeling was soon overtaken by concern at the situation. It was concluded that the secretary had not made lodgements on all the monies received into her care. It was decided that the secretary had some explaining to do and, in that context, the principal wrote and posted a registered letter to the claimant dated 24th March 2009.

The Principal wrote to the secretary about "considerable discrepancies to accounts" and invited her to attend a meeting. The first paragraph of that letter read as follows:

"On checking the accounts with our Accountant it appears that there are considerable discrepancies to accounts that you were dealing with whilst you were working with the school".

That letter then invited the claimant to attend a meeting with the principal and the accountant *"in order to clarify and hopefully explain the discrepancies so that the books can be finalised"*.

That letter also informed its intended recipient *"we have no option but to suspend you on full pay..."*. The principal explained the "we" meant the respondent as she felt she had the authority to act in this way without consulting the respondent.

The meeting was attended by the secretary, the school principal, the accountant, & others resulting in disciplinary procedures being invoked against the secretary.

Another meeting was requested, and agreed to, where the secretary denied stealing money from school.

She was told that there were nine charges against her and a letter listed those. Her representative asked if there was a report, but the respondent would not confirm or deny that there was a report. The meeting was unsatisfactory, and the respondent representatives would not confirm or deny if the accountant had a report.

The claimant was asked directly by her representative if she stole money from her employer, and she replied *"No"*. She was also asked if she had resisted answering questions by her employer, and she replied

"No". It was put to her that a lack of information left her unable to answer questions, and she agreed that this was the case. She had no access to her own office records, and if she had she would have been able to answer questions. If she had access to the information "it would never have come to this".

The secretary would only answer questions if she could return to work as this was in-line with her contract and disciplinary conditions. She felt that she had already been sacked.

She got a letter from the school to say that she was not willing to answer questions. She expected to have a meeting with the BOM. The next letter she received was on 5th June, 2009 and she was asked if she would answer questions. The next letter that she got was a letter of dismissal.

She felt that she had no recourse to an appeal of her dismissal as the letter did not mention this.

EAT Decision
The EAT found in the secretary's favour and deemed the dismissal unfair. The Tribunal accepted that there were discrepancies in school monies and noted that the audit found a shortfall of €12,000 in school monies. It recognised that there were legitimate questions to be asked, but said the school was not entitled to single out the secretary as other people had access to the monies, and the accounting measures adopted by all members of staff were *'very slack'*.

It then applied the *"test of reasonableness"*:

"As a matter of law, the Tribunal when considering whether, or not, the particular action or inaction of an employee justifies a dismissal will have regard to the reasonableness of the employer's decision to dismiss. In deciding whether, or not, the dismissal was unfair we apply a test of reasonableness to

1. The nature and extent of the enquiry carried out by the respondent prior to the decision to dismiss the claimant,

and 2. The conclusion arrived at by the respondent that, on the basis of the information, resulting from such enquiry, the claimant should be dismissed.

In this particular case, the quality and extent of the respondent's investigation was highly questionable in circumstances, where the accounting practices in place were very relaxed, certain other persons had access to the monies and one individual, namely, the principal was given too much responsibility for the conduct of the enquiry and the instigation of the disciplinary procedure. However, that is not the end of the matter as the claimant herself has some responsibility to bear. The claimant received advice that she should not attend a disciplinary meeting unless she was first reinstated. Her refusal to engage with the process effectively backed the respondent into a corner. If the facts of this case were different, this failure to engage would have entitled the respondent to dismiss her as it would have had little alternative. However, it is a unique feature of this case that the initial contact between the respondent and the claimant's family was handled poorly and it is also a feature of this case that the enquiry itself was flawed to such an extent that it would be unjust to hold that her failure to engage remedies the deficiencies on the respondent's part.

In those circumstances, the decision to dismiss, based as it was on a flawed enquiry could not be said to be within the range of reasonable responses open to the employer.

The Tribunal determines that compensation, and not reinstatement, be the most appropriate remedy in this case. Accordingly, having regard to all the circumstances, the Tribunal awards the claimant the sum of €9,850.00."

LESSON

This case provides another good example of "the test of reasonableness" that the Employment Appeals Tribunal applies to the conduct of the employer when deciding whether a dismissal was unfair or not. It is vitally important that the employer afford fully natural justice and fair procedures in disciplinary proceedings, particularly where the outcome is dismissal and loss of income.

Read the full decision here: http://employmentlawireland.ie/wp-content/uploads/2013/04/school-secretary.pdf

Pregnant Woman who Suffered Still Birth Awarded €72,000 for Unfair Dismissal

In this case, a pregnant woman, who suffered the loss of her baby by stillbirth, brought a case for constructive dismissal due to unacceptable treatment at the hands of her employer.

The claimant alleged that she was asked by the employer to compromise her professional ethics, and that she was treated unacceptably in respect of her pregnancy.

The EAT heard that the employer was unhappy that the pregnancy would lead to maternity leave, and increased her work load during her pregnancy.

The employer also told her it would need to shorten her maternity leave as it could not do without her, and the claimant received texts and emails while in hospital after suffering a serious bleed incident.

When discharged from hospital, she was collected at the hospital and ferried back to work.

Her baby died on July 1 and subsequently delivered on July 4, 2010 but her employer insisted she return to work on July 19 on a part-time basis. A week later her employer insisted she work full-time.

She was subjected to indecent comments after the still birth and the employer terminated a part time work agreement.

The EAT found that the employer showed a total disregard for claimant's well being.

The EAT was told that the company intended to replace her, and the company director refused to discuss or engage with the claimant, who left the employment and brought a claim for constructive dismissal under the Unfair Dismissals Acts.

Normally, a constructive dismissal claim is a difficult one to win because the employee must prove he/she had no option but to leave due to the conduct of the employer.

In this case the EAT awarded €72,000 for unfair dismissal.

Lesson

The EAT found that the claimant was treated in a *"wholly inappropriate manner in respect of her pregnancy"*, and she was *"inundated with work-related texts and emails"* when in hospital after suffering a serious bleed. It also found that the employer insisted she return to work soon after the death of her baby, and then insisted she return to full time work.

In these circumstances, the finding of unfair dismissal and a substantial award was not surprising.

6. Time Limits

Employer Loses Appeal against Rights Commissioner Award of €8,000 Wages Due to Employee

This case demonstrates the need to take seriously the time limits set down in the legislation for appeals.

A Rights Commissioner decision of 5th June, 2010 under the Payment Of Wages Act 1991, had awarded €8,000 in respect of wages due under company sick pay scheme.

The employer had 6 weeks within which to lodge an appeal. An appeal dated 22nd July, 2010 was lodged by the employer but only received by the Employment Appeals Tribunal on 4th August, 2011.

The EAT stated:

"The Payment of Wages Act 1991 states that appeals are to be initiated within 6 weeks of decision.

The Tribunal is not satisfied that the appeal was lodged in time. It is mandatory to lodge the appeal within six weeks and no discretion is allowed. The Tribunal does not have jurisdiction to hear the case.

The Employment Appeals Tribunal found that the appeal was not lodged in time, and the Tribunal had no discretion to hear the case. Accordingly it affirmed the decision of the Rights Commissioner to award €8,000 to the claimant."

Lesson

Time limits laid down in much of the employment related legislation are strict-and are generally 6 months, and possibly 12 months in exceptional circumstances-and the EAT/Rights Commissioner Service do not have the power or discretion to hear appeals outside those time limits.

Read the full decision here: http://employmentlawireland.ie/wp-content/uploads/2013/04/payment-of-wages-1991.pdf

7. Redundancy

Construction Worker's Claim of Unfair Selection for Redundancy Fails

This case involved a construction worker who claimed he was unfairly selected for redundancy, and/or that it was not a genuine redundancy situation. If he could prove this he would win his case for unfair dismissal.

The Employment Appeals Tribunal heard that the worker had provided long service since 1998. He was firstly placed on 3 day week, and then told that he was to be made redundant.

There was no appeal mechanism to the decision. He requested copy of the selection process but never received it.

He argued at the EAT that the redundancy process should be on the basis of last in first out.

He had accepted a sum of €5,000 plus statutory redundancy, and the EAT heard that he earned €80,000 per year.

His case was that he was not redundant insofar as it was not a genuine redundancy, and/or he was unfairly selected for redundancy.

The EAT found that the redundancy was fair, and for the claim of unfair selection to apply there must be workers in similar employment. This was not the case here.

The EAT heard that there was no recognised procedure for redundancy with a trade union in this case, and that last in, first out did not apply according to employer.

The EAT decided that there could be no finding of unfair selection, and that it was a genuine redundancy under Redundancy Payments Acts 1967 as amended, therefore his unfair dismissal claim failed.

LESSON

This case is one which was based on a claim of either the redundancy being an unfair selection, and/or it was a sham redundancy, that is not a genuine one. The unfair selection argument could not stand up because there were no other workers in similar employment.

If the claimant could have shown that it was a sham redundancy, then the claim of unfair dismissal was an avenue open to him. However, the EAT found it was a real redundancy and his claim failed.

8. Bullying and Workplace/Occupational Stress

Bullied in Primary School-Special Needs Assistant Awarded €255,000

This case involved a claim based on bullying in a primary school by an employee of the school- special needs assistant.

This case was brought int High Court and was based on the non physical personal injury suffered by the special needs assistant.

The High Court decided that the Board of Management of St Anne's National School in the Curragh, Kildare undermined the employee's dignity at work by its "severe" and "unmerited" treatment of her.

The Judge described the school Principal's account of the complaint against the SNA as "almost certainly untrue".

The Judge also held that the Principal of the School *"trumped up"* another complaint against the SNA.

As a result of her treatment in the workplace, the Court held that the SNA suffered a definite and identifiable psychiatric injury.

The breakdown of the award was €140,276 for loss of earnings (past and future) and €115,000 for the personal injury.

After an incident involving the locking of the door of the school's "sensory room", the school Principal, Pauline Dempsey, brought the SNA to a meeting and warned her of disciplinary action.

However, she later wrote to the SNA advising her that no action would be taken. Nevertheless, there would be a three month review of the SNA's performance.

The review of the SNA's work involved the filling in of a review form, which led to a difficulty with the Principal accusing the SNA of a *"falsification"* of the review form.

The Principal then brought the original incident involving the locked door and the performance of the SNA to the Board of Management. The Board recommended that the SNA receive a formal warning and that her next salary increment be deferred.

The Judge in the High Court doubted that the Principal had outlined the full facts surrounding the difficulty to the Board.

The Principal then gave the SNA a letter stating that an investigation had been carried out, and if there was a further breach of school policy there could be further action including dismissal.

The High Court held that there was no such investigation, and that the SNA had been subjected to a disciplinary sanction that was severe and unmerited.

Lesson

Employers need to be very careful to afford fair procedures to all employees, regardless of their position, status, or seniority.

They also need to be aware that Courts are becoming more prepared to recognise non physical injuries eg stress in the workplace.

And, a High Court decision going against the employer is not confined to the award being limited to 2 years' salary as with unfair dismissals legislation, not to mention the significant costs of High Court proceedings.

Read the full High Court decision here:
http://www.courts.ie/Judgments.nsf/09859e7a3f34669680256ef300 4a27de/26389732f9add42380257cde0030df7d?OpenDocument

Bullying and Workplace Stress as a Personal Injury-A Notable High Court Decision in 2014

A March, 2014 judgment in the High Court, in the case *Glynn v Minister for Justice Equality and Law Reform (2014 IEHC 135)*, is well worth looking at, because it deals with workplace stress, bullying, and personal injury claims in the workplace.

The claimant was a civil servant and worked in Gort Garda station in Co. Galway. Her claim was that she suffered stress as a result of pressure placed on her in 2005 to complete monthly accounts for the Garda station.

Prior to this incident there were other incidents-not getting on with a Garda who she felt was constantly checking on her-going back to 1996 and she had taken sick leave in November of that year.

She returned on a 3 day week in 1997. In 2004 she was promoted to the position of Finance Officer.

In May, 2005 she worked on the accounts for 4 days during which she claimed to have suffered considerable stress.

She then raised, with Garda Headquarters, her concerns about a cheque for expenses in favour of the Superintendent. She claimed the Superintendent told her he would take her job from her if she didn't do what he told her.

She then went on sick leave for 6 months, and returned when the Superintendent had retired from the station.

In cross-examination, the claimant admitted that she had suffered from depression prior to the incidents complained of. She also had failed to contact the Employment Assistance Services of the Department of Justice in 1996 in relation to her bullying allegation.

The defence case was that there was no bullying, and the Superintendent had no issues with her, nor was there a problem with the expenses cheque.

The Legal Issues and Principles
The High Court, Justice Kearns, observed:

".....bullying, workplace stress and occupational stress are all things which, conceptually at least, are quite different from each other, though on occasion they can overlap and coincide. Occupational stress is not actionable given that occupational stress is something which every employed person may experience at some stage of his or her working life and can occur for reasons quite distinct from and unrelated to bullying....."

The Court noted that workplace stress can be actionable if certain criteria are met. However, it is different from bullying insofar as it lacks the degree of deliberateness associated with bullying.

"Workplace stress can also be the result of negligence where excessive demands are made of an employee or where complaints about shortcomings in the workplace go unheeded. It lacks however that degree of deliberateness which is the hallmark of bullying".

The Court said the following question should be asked in relation to the claim of bullying:

"whether the behaviour complained of, by reference to an objective test, imports that degree of calibrated inappropriateness and repetition which differentiates bullying from workplace stress or occupational stress"

It also referred to the legal definition of bullying set out in *Industrial Relations Act 1990 (Code of Practice Detailing Procedures for Addressing Bullying in the Workplace) (Declaration) Order 2002 (S.I. No. 17 of 2002)* viz *"repeated inappropriate behaviour, direct or indirect, whether verbal, physical or otherwise, conducted by one or more persons against another or others, at the place of work and/or in the course of employment, which could reasonably be regarded as undermining the individual's right to dignity at work. An isolated incident of the behaviour described in this definition may be an affront to dignity at work but, as a once off incident, it is not considered to be bullying."*

The Court noted that this definition required an objective test to decide whether bullying had occurred.

The Court referred to *Quigley v Complex Tooling and Moulding Ltd [2009] 1 I.R. 349*, and the acceptance by the Supreme Court in that case of the definition of bullying or harassment at work, as set out in S.I. No. 17 of 2002 above.

Justice Kearns observed that the relevant legal principles for workplace stress were laid down in *Berber v Dunnes Stores [2009] E.L.R. 61*, (which accepted the practical propositions set out in the 2002 case *Hatton V Sutherland [2002] 2 All E.R.1*).

Mr. Justice Kearns stated:

"These legal principles are:

1. The ordinary principles of employer's liability apply.

2. The threshold question is whether the kind of harm to the particular employee was reasonably foreseeable: this has two components (a) an injury to health (as distinct from occupational stress) which (b) is attributable to stress at work (as distinct from other factors).

3. Foreseeability depends upon what the employer knows (or ought reasonably to know) about the individual employee. Because of the nature of mental disorder it is harder to foresee than physical injury, but may be easier to foresee in a known individual than in the population at large. An employer is usually entitled to assume that the employee can withstand the normal pressures of the job, unless he knows of some particular problem or vulnerability.

4. The employer is generally entitled to take what he is told by his employee (including what he is told by the employee's medical adviser) at face value unless there is good reason to think to the contrary.

5. The indications of impending harm to health arising from stress at work must be plain enough for any reasonable employer to realise that he should do something about it.

6. The employer is only in breach of duty if he has failed to take the steps which are reasonable in the circumstances, bearing in mind the magnitude of the risk of harm occurring, the gravity of the harm which may occur, the cost and practicability of preventing it, and the justifications for running the risk.

7. An employer can only reasonably be expected to take steps which are likely to do some good: the court is likely to need expert evidence on this.

8. If the only reasonable and effective steps would have been to dismiss or demote the employee the employer will not be in breach of duty in allowing a willing employee to continue in the job.

9. In all cases it is necessary to identify the steps which the employer both could and should have taken before finding him in breach of his duty of care.

10. The claimant must show that the breach of duty caused or materially contributed to the harm suffered. It is not enough to show that occupational stress has caused the harm."

The Decision
The High Court held that 2 things exercised the plaintiff:

1. a sense of injustice that she, as a civilian employee, was not being paid the same rate as a Garda colleague and

2. the working conditions she had to work in in 1996 (in a portacabin/temporary accommodation).

The Court also observed that there was no acceptable explanation by the plaintiff as to why she did not disclose a prior history of depression, and accepted that the Superintendent's evidence was reliable and credible.

Justice Kearns stated that he could not see that anything in the behaviour of the Garda colleague or Superintendent constituted bullying or harassment.

Furthermore

"the events upon which the plaintiff relies to mount her claim turn on the events of a few short days in May, 2005 a time span more identifiable with a once-off or single incident rather than the kind of 'repetitive' and 'inappropriate' conduct which constitutes the wrong of workplace bullying or harassment".

The court concluded that the plaintiff had not made a case for bullying or workplace stress causing or contributing to foreseeable injury or damage. She had no complaints of workplace stress for the eight years between 1997 and 2005.

Justice Kearns went further and said

"Even if mistaken on these issues I would also be of the view that the plaintiff failed to demonstrate that her stress was attributable to the matters she complained of in this case. She had a prior history of stress and depression which was not disclosed until it was uncovered through the discovery process. I believe any subsequent stresses suffered by the plaintiff were attributable both to life events (including the tragic death of her nephew and the death of her father) and, in 2005, to occupational stress only".

Lesson

For an employee to win a case for a personal injury brought on by workplace stress, three things must be looked at:

1) has the employee suffered an injury to his health, as opposed to mere "ordinary occupational stress"?

2) was that injury attributable to stress at work, as distinct from other factors outside the workplace?

3) was the injury forseeable, that is, should the employer have foreseen the injury, based on what he knew about the employee?

Read the full High Court decision:
http://courts.ie/Judgments.nsf/0/E0F985DFA4C6594780257CA2003930E3

9. Independent Contractor or Employee?

The Crucial Significance in an Unfair Dismissal Case

When a person brings a claim for unfair dismissal under the unfair dismissal legislation, there is one essential proof that they must establish at the outset: they must prove they were an employee.

In most cases this is clear and is not a problem.

But if the employer can show that the person was an independent contractor, and not an employee, then it is *"game over"* and the case cannot go ahead as an unfair dismissal case.

You would imagine by now that the law surrounding whether someone was an employee or independent contractor, that is self employed, or not, would be clear.

But this question continues to be litigated in the Employment Appeals Tribunal and the Courts.

This occurred again in a High Court case in May, 2014-*Murphy -v- Grand Circle Travel [2014] IEHC 337* .

Sabina Murphy had been dismissed from her job with Grand Circle Travel and brought a case for unfair dismissal to the EAT. It decided that she was not an employee but an independent contractor and found against her.

Murphy appealed her case to the Circuit Court and was awarded compensation of €50,900 plus costs.

Grand Circle Travel appealed this decision to the High Court, and central to their case was an independent contractor agreement signed by both parties.

Murphy claimed she was pressured into signing this agreement without independent legal advice, but the High Court Judge found it difficult to believe that someone who had conducted her case so well as a lay litigant could have been cowed into signing the agreement:

I do not readily see a lady who has sturdily asserted her rights before the Defendant and the legal system meekly assenting to the signed endorsement of a document expressly purporting to commit her to a regime fundamentally at variance with her perception of her engagement already then over several months.

Justice Moriarty, in coming to his decision, stated:

"I have carefully considered all the matters which seem to me to throw light upon the nature of the relationship between the parties, including any documentation purporting to record that nature, in addition to correspondence and memoranda relating to daily dealings during the three seasons of engagement, and documentation recording remuneration and other financial dealings between them. It is well settled from the Irish and English case-law cited that controversies of this nature can rarely be resolved by an aggregation of documentation all pointing utterly unequivocally to one conclusion or the other.

I have come to the view that the overall probabilities, including my feeling that the Plaintiff's work over the three years involved a degree of engagement by tourism entities other than the Defendant in excess of the small incidence she referred to in evidence, warrant a finding that the relationship was that of an independent contractor."

Lesson

Whether someone is an employee or independent contractor is, therefore, not a simple academic argument; it is vital in determining the outcome of many unfair dismissal cases.

If the claimant is not an employee, an unfair dismissal claim is dead in the water.

However, commencing legal proceedings for breach of contract may be an option.

Read the full High Court decision:
http://courts.ie/Judgments.nsf/bce24a8184816f1580256ef30048ca50/8f8892f7451a052480257d11003443c8?OpenDocument

10. Settlement Agreements

Avoid This Costly Mistake in Your Employment Settlement Agreement

The case of *Joan Healy and Michael Healy against Bia Ganbreise Teoranta* demonstrates the danger of relying on standard, or template type, documents in the workplace.

This case involved the effectiveness of a settlement agreement to prevent future claims arising from the employment.

This is a common type of agreement used to settle many employment related disputes.

It is also used when making an employee redundant, and intends to provide protection for the employer from future claims by that employee.

In this case the appellants, Joan and Michael Healy, sold their business to company F in 2008, and commenced working with F.

In September, 2010 the Healys issued Circuit Court proceedings against Co. F claiming damages for breach of contract for failure to pay each of the appellants certain wages.

In 2011, the Healys compromised their Circuit Court claim after their employment had ceased with F and they were offered new employment with X, which, with F, had bought the entire share capital of A, a subsidiary of F.

When they compromised their claim the settlement agreement contained a "full and final settlement" clause which is common in these types of agreement. The settlement sum was €31,750 in respect of unpaid wages for a 2 year period.

In 2012, X placed the Healys on a temporary layoff. They in turn served a RP9 form claiming redundancy payments from X.

X informed the Healys that their positions in X were redundant, and no suitable alternative positions were available.

In July, 2012, the Healys initiated appeals under the Redundancy Payments Acts with the Employment Appeals Tribunal, with each appellant seeking a redundancy lump sum payment from the respondent.

The respondent contended that the Employment Appeals Tribunal had no jurisdiction to hear the appeals under the Redundancy Payments Acts 1967 to 2007 by virtue of the settlement agreements, in particular by virtue of clauses 7 &13 thereof.

X also contended that, in any event, the appellants did not have the requisite two years' service to entitle them to a redundancy lump sum payment.

Section 51 of Redundancy Payments Act 1967

51.—Any provision in an agreement (whether a contract of employment or not) shall be void in so far as it purports to exclude or limit the operation of any provision of this Act.

However, the Tribunal accepted that it was well accepted that this does not preclude severance agreements or agreements compromising claims containing such exclusions.

The settlement agreements in this case contained these 2 clauses:

"Clause 7
The Employee agrees that the terms of the Agreement provide a full and final settlement of the proceedings and all or any claims that he/she has or may have against the company and /or the employer and/or any of their respective group of companies, officers and/or employees agents and shareholders, howsoever arising, including, without limitation,

arising out of or in connection with the employment of the Employee of the company and /or the employer and /or any of their respective Group companies, and the employee hereby fully and finally releases all such entities from all or and any such claims, whether in statute or common law in tort, in equity or otherwise howsoever arising

Clause 13
This Agreement shall enure to the benefit of and be binding upon the respective parties hereto and their respective personal representatives and successors."

In Hurley v the Royal Yacht Club [1997] ELR 225 Buckley J.,in the Circuit Court, considered a waiver clause in an agreement in the context of the Unfair Dismissals Acts and, having concluded that there must be informed consent to such a waiver, later in his judgement set out what this requires:

"I am satisfied that the applicant was entitled to be advised of his entitlements under the employment protection legislation and that any agreement or compromise should have listed the various Acts which were applicable, or at least made it clear that they had been taken into account by the employee. I am also satisfied that the applicant should have been advised in writing that he should take appropriate advice as to his rights, which presumably in this case, would have been legal advice. In the absence of such advice I find the agreement to be void"

This statement of the law was applied by Smyth J. the High Court in *Sunday Newspapers Ltd v Kinsella and Brady [2008] ELR 53.*

In this case, the Tribunal accepted that the Healys were legally advised and gave their informed consent to the waiver.

However, Clause 7 of the settlement agreements neither lists the various Acts under which the appellants might have waived their entitlements, nor does it make clear that they had been taken into account by the appellants.

The unsworn and uncontested evidence on behalf of the appellants was that the unpaid wages of the appellants was the only issue discussed in the negotiations leading to the settlement agreement. This fact is corroborated by a number of other uncontested facts: the settlement figure of €31,750.00 was the precise amount of the unpaid wages owing to the appellants; payslips dated 30 July 2011 in this amount with the usual deductions made therefrom were issued to each of the appellants, and the respondent's letter of 23 September 2011 to the Office of the Revenue Commissioners confirming that the payment was in respect of a number of weeks worked in 2009-2011

The Tribunal found that there was no break in the appellants' employment between 7 July 2011 and 16 July 2011 and that on the purchase of the entire share capital of Co A by Co X in May 2011, the rights of the employees remained unaffected.

Similarly, a change of company name does not affect those rights.

"Accordingly, for the above reasons the Tribunal finds that the appellants did not waive their statutory entitlement to a redundancy lump sum payment, their employment had been continuous from the time they became employees on 8 July 2008 until it was terminated by reason of redundancy on or around 22 March 2012."

Lesson

I have come across many standard "template" type forms which employers are using when they are paying redundancy to an employee.

This case shows the importance of having a properly drafted settlement agreement in settling any claim or paying off an employee by way of redundancy. Don't cut off your nose to spite your face when it comes to settling an employment related, or any, claim. Get legal advice. It will prove to be money well spent.

Read the full decision here:
http://www.workplacerelations.ie/en/Cases/2014/October/RP493_2012_RP494_2012.html

About the Author

Terry Gorry is a solicitor and small business owner. He has built and run a wide range of businesses in Ireland since 1986. So, he has a unique insight into issues facing small business owner, employers, and employees. There are not too many problems you will come across that he hasn't encountered. He helps employers and employees with their legal issues, especially employment law. Learn more about his services at any of his websites:

http://EmploymentRightsIreland.com

http://BusinessAndLegal.ie

http://SmallBusinessLawIreland.com

Other books by Terry Gorry

Employment Law in Ireland-A Guide in Plain English for Employers and Employees, available on Amazon.com/Amazon.co.uk.

Thank You, and One Last Thing

Thank you for purchasing this book. I really appreciate it.To help me write books that help you and people like you, I would welcome any feedback you have.

Where, and how, can the book be improved?

What other topics would you like to read about?

Amazon Review

If you enjoyed this book, I would really appreciate it if you left a review on Amazon.com.

This url: http://goo.gl/cliHDw takes you directly to leave your review on Amazon. This gives me great encouragement, and helps others who might be helped by the information in my books.

Thanks.

Terry Gorry, 2015

Thanks.

Printed in Great Britain
by Amazon